Sylvia

A remarkable life

Nolan Thaxton Cordle

Moonshell Books, Inc.
California

Sylvia / Nolan Thaxton Cordle—1st ed.

For my wife, always

Love is not love
Which alters when it alteration finds,
Or bends with the remover to remove.
O no! it is an ever-fixed mark
That looks on tempests and is never shaken…

—SHAKESPEARE, SONNET 116

FOREWORD

Sylvia Cordle, my wife and soul mate, is now suffering from dementia in a special home, where she needs round-the-clock care. She is the most remarkable person I have ever known. Born in Cuba and raised to a life of privilege, she survived a revolution. She and her family fled to America, going from privilege to poverty overnight.

Though we were childless, she spent her life helping children, and changing the paradigm everywhere she worked. Through it all, she never spoke to her friends of all she had accomplished. She was modest to a fault.

For this reason, I believe it is most important that her life and accomplishments be documented. I want her friends to really know about her. While I'm sure that all who know her realize that she has an extremely intelligent mind and a most likeable personality, still, what she did with her life will hopefully surprise and delight them.

I have used the names of real people when it is appropriate, and used their titles when it is not.

—Nolan Thaxton Cordle
July 2016

To Neil
My Dear Friend

Nolan

CHAPTER ONE

Cuba

The island of Cuba was discovered by Europeans on October 28, 1492, when Cristobal Colon (Christopher Columbus) landed. He named the island Juana, the first of several subsequent names. Finally it was called Cuba, a variant of the aboriginal name: Cubanascan.

Columbus declared Cuba to be "the most beautiful earth that human eye has ever seen." Cuba truly is beautiful. The island was inhabited by various Mesoamerican cultures prior to the arrival of Columbus. After that, it became a Spanish colony, ruled by a Spanish governor in Havana.

In 1762, Havana was briefly occupied by England, before being returned to Spain in exchange for Florida. A series of rebellions during the 19th century failed to end Spanish rule. However, the Spanish-American War resulted in a Spanish withdrawal from the island in 1898, and Cuba gained its formal independence in 1902.

Before the Spanish left the island, they established rice and tobacco as its primary crops. Large numbers of field laborers were required, so African slaves were imported to satisfy this need. Later, with the expansion of slavery, Cuban sugar plantations became the most important world producer of sugar.

Many slaves rebelled throughout the 19th century, causing many deaths of slaves and their masters. Following all these rebellions, all slavery was abolished by 1886, making Cuba the second-to-last country in the western hemisphere to abolish slavery. Many Cubans were worn out by all the turmoil due to rebellions, and made overtures to the United States for annexation. Each time the subject was brought up by the U.S. government, though, it was rejected. However, in time this mood of rejection was replaced by a desire to bring Cuba under the control of the U.S. when many Americans came to believe that the Cuban people's continued battle with Spain was grounds for intervention. The U.S. government offered to buy Cuba in 1898, but was turned down by the Spanish government.

In 1898, the U.S. government sent the battleship *Maine* to Havana harbor to protect "the lives of Americans living in Havana." Unfortunately, *Maine* was destroyed by an explosion, which killed 268 crewmembers. Congress declared war on Spain to "liberate" Cuba.

The Spanish-American War was over in short order and liberated not only Cuba, but also the Philippines. Within a short time, the Cuban economy was dominated by American capital. By 1902, Americans controlled 80 percent of Cuba's sugar and cigar factories.

In 1902, the United States handed over control to a Cuban government. The remainder of the twentieth century would be one of turmoil and growth for the new nation of Cuba.

In 1940, Fulgencio Batista was elected President. The Cuban constitution denied Batista the possibility of running for a consecutive term in the 1944 election.

In 1952, Batista seized power in a coup three months before the civic elections were to be held. Although corruption was rife under Batista, Cuba flourished economically during his regime. An eight-hour day had been established in 1933, and according to the International Labor Organization, in 1958 the average industrial salary in Cuba was the world's eighth highest and the average agricultural wage was higher than in developed nations such as Denmark, West Germany, Belgium, or France. In the 1950s, Cuba's gross domestic product (GDP) per capita was roughly equal to that of contemporary Italy and higher than Japan. In addition, there was a large middle class. Cuba had the fifth highest number of televisions per capita in the world and the healthcare system was remarkably developed. By the late 1950s, it had one of the highest numbers of doctors—more even than England. According to the World Health Organization, Cuba had the lowest infant mortality rate in Latin America and the 13th lowest rate in the world—better than France, Belgium, West Germany, Israel, Japan, Austria, Italy, Spain, and Portugal.

If all this was true, how then did Castro take over and establish a communist government that destroyed the economy and personal freedom? This is an incredibly important question, and one that is not entirely answerable by scholars and historians.

CHAPTER TWO

Sylvia

She was born Silvia Albertina Caballero Bilbao on November 3, 1940, in Havana, Cuba, which was then considered the "Paris of the Caribbean." Her parents were Alberto and Josefina Caballero. Her father was an attorney and the owner of a fertilizer factory that sold its product all over North and South America. His favorite place to travel was to the lakes of

upstate New York.

Sylvia (she chose the American spelling of her name) was born into privilege. However, she was not spoiled. Her parents, being good Catholics, gave her a sense of responsibility toward her less fortunate countrymen. Through their church, Sylvia participated in helping the needy.

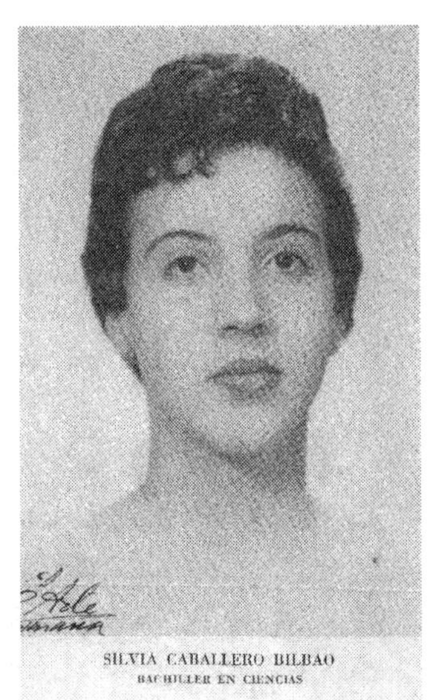

SILVIA CABALLERO BILBAO
BACHILLER EN CIENCIAS

For the first 18 years of her life, Sylvia was by all accounts a happy, well-adjusted child and teenager. At five years of age, she was enrolled in a private school, the Instituto Edison, which gave all classes in English. She attended from the first grade to the twelfth and graduated at the age of 16.

Sylvia had animals—dogs and cats. But her favorite animal was a goat. She loved that goat and the goat loved her. She named him Papeto, and he followed her around like a puppy.

Her home was very large and Sylvia had her own room with a TV and a radio. As a teenager, she would listen to rock and roll over the American radio stations broadcasting from Miami and other cities along the coast. Sylvia's understanding of English allowed her to enjoy radio and TV from Florida.

Sylvia's parents, especially her father, wanted her to be a doctor. In all fairness, Alberto didn't really care if she actually practiced as a physician, but he wanted her to have *Dr.* in front of her name. He should be forgiven for this attitude—Alberto was a product of his time and place. In his culture, women did not participate to any degree in a man's world. While it was fine to have a title, the upper-class ladies in Cuba were expected only to be supportive of their men.

For two years, Sylvia attended pre-med classes at the University of Havana, fairly certain that her life was laid out by her parents and that circumstances would allow her to enjoy continued privilege and happiness.

But something was on the horizon that would change her life and that of her parents forever, and send this privileged young woman into a life of challenge and struggle, but one that would enable her to do wonderful things for her fellow man.

CHAPTER THREE

The Revolution

In 1952, Fidel Castro, a young lawyer running for a seat in the Chamber of Representatives, circulated a petition to depose Batista's government on the grounds that it had illegitimately suspended the electoral process. However, the courts did not act on the petition and ignored Castro's legal challenges. Castro thus resolved to use armed force to overthrow Batista.

Castro and his brother Raul gathered supporters, and on July 26, 1953, led an attack on an army barracks near Santiago. The attack ended in failure. The authorities killed several of the insurgents, captured Fidel and Raul, tried them both, and sentenced them to fifteen years in prison.

However, Batista released both men after two years. Fidel and Raul were exiled to Mexico, where they met the Argentine revolutionary Ernesto "Che" Guevara. The three of them organized the 26th of July Movement with the goal of overthrowing Batista.

In December 1956, Fidel Castro led a group of 82 fighters to Cuba on a small yacht that was meant to support only 20 people. They landed, but Batista's forces killed or captured most of Castro's men. Fidel, Raul, and Che escaped to the Sierra Maestra mountains with 12 others of his forces. Fidel Castro was able to continue his guerrilla campaign, supported by well-armed groups with the same intent—to depose Batista.

As time passed, and the rebels under Castro grew stronger, multiple attempts by Batista's forces to crush the insurgents ended in failure. The United States imposed trade restrictions on Batista and sent an envoy, who attempted to persuade Batista to leave the country voluntarily. With his military situation becoming untenable, Batista fled on January 1, 1959, and Fidel Castro took over.

Immediately upon taking control, Castro moved to consolidate his power by brutally marginalizing other resistance groups and executing those who did not agree with him. By the end of

1960, all opposition newspapers had been closed down and all radio and television stations had come under state control. Teachers and other professionals found to harbor ill will toward Castro were shot or sent to jail.

Raul Castro became the commander of the Revolutionary Armed Forces and set up a system of neighborhood watchdogs to spy on and report anyone speaking ill of Castro or the revolution.

Castro's government expropriated all foreign companies owning property and businesses in Cuba, notably the United Fruit Company and the International Telephone and Telegraph Company. Thousands of Americans lost farms and property they had owned for 40 years.

Hundreds of thousands of Cubans began to flee the island, eventually forming exile communities in the United States.

Granted, Batista was not a good man and most certainly did bad things to his enemies. Still, the Cuban people had been doing well, with the largest middle class in Latin America. The people had freedom and could start companies, making a living on their own terms. And yet, Castro walked right in and took it all away. There is evidence that the U.S. government played a role in Batista's downfall, as did newspapers such as the *New York Times* and *Time* magazine, which made heroes of

Castro and a dozen men hiding out in the mountains.

*

In 1958, when Castro came down from the mountains and marched into Havana, Alberto, Sylvia's father, told the family that this was nothing more than another petty dictator taking over and soon all would be back to normal. That was what a lot of Cubans thought.

Sylvia became aware that all was not well in Cuba as classes at the University of Havana were becoming poorly attended or even canceled. Further, Alberto found himself without his business when the Revolutionary Guard came to his factory and took over. He was allowed to stay on as a janitor. The family was also informed that their home was too large for only three people and that they would be moved, in due time, to a smaller unit. Sylvia was about to experience the most shocking experience of her young life—one that would haunt her for the remainder of her life.

Sylvia continued to attend classes in hopes that she would be able to complete the four-year degree and move on to get her doctorate. However, that was coming to an end.

One sunny day, the Revolutionary Guard invaded her class. With machine guns aimed, they ordered a few of the students to one side of the room and held a "trial." Those few separated from the rest of the class were judged guilty of counter-revolutionary behavior, because they had been heard to speak unfavorably about Castro. They were executed with machine guns in front of the rest of the class.

Sylvia's best friend was cut in half by a rain of concentrated fire. In complete shock, Sylvia never attended another class.

More shock was to come. The Revolutionary Guard, under orders from Castro, rounded up 75,000 selected citizens, including the Caballero family. Packed with the others into a Havana stadium, Sylvia witnessed two hundred people tried and executed by firing squads.

Their neighbor, a doctor, owned a rifle from the Spanish-American War that did not even work. It had been his grandfather's from that war. Sylvia and her parents heard a commotion outside and went out to see what was happening. Apparently someone had notified the Revolutionary Guard of the fact that the doctor had failed to turn in the non-operational gun. The man was dragged out of his house and executed in front of the Caballero family and the neighborhood. Sylvia witnessed her neighbor, whom she had known all of her young life, murdered. She never forgot that sight, nor all the other bloody murders she had witnessed by ruthless men who seemed to have regressed to the point of enjoying the act of killing anyone who looked at them sideways, of taking any excuse to shed blood. By this time, Sylvia was numb in mind and body.

For the remainder of the time they spent in Cuba, Alberto made it clear that his wife, Josefina, and Sylvia were not to speak negatively to anyone about Castro or the revolution.

One of Alberto's special talents was his ability to make people like him, and this included the Revolutionary Guard and others. He did not hide from them. On the contrary, he deliberately found reasons to be around them. He complimented them and let them know that he agreed with their taking over his company. Alberto's motivation, of course, was to keep his wife and daughter as safe as possible.

Cubans were fleeing their country by the hundreds and eventually by the thousands, so President Lyndon Johnson declared that any Cuban who could wade ashore to the United States would be considered a political refugee. Over the next two years, the Caballero family caused no problems for Castro. In fact, the Castro regime was so busy trying to collect all the guns and kill anyone who resisted that they did not move the Caballeros from their home as they had promised.

Alberto did not want to risk trying to get his wife and daughter to Florida by illegally slipping out in the middle of the night on a small boat. He was a charming man who could generally get his way with almost anyone. Eventually, by 1961 he received approval to emigrate to the United States. The family were only allowed to take the clothes they had on and a small bag of personal items. They could take no money. As they left their home for the last time to go to the airport, Russian "technicians" were waiting at the end of the walkway to occupy their beloved home.

Surprisingly, Pan Am was still taking passengers approved by the new regime to the United States. But as Sylvia walked ahead of her parents through the gate to board the airliner, the guard closed the gate and refused to allow her parents to board with her. So this emotionally battered young woman with next to no luggage had to board the Pan Am flight in tears, not knowing what was to become of her parents or what awaited her in Miami.

What awaited her was fear of the unknown. Sylvia had always had family, relatives, and friends to support her, and now she was all alone, living in a barracks with strangers, with not even a change of clothes, minimal food, and to some degree minimal protection and health care. She lived on peanut butter. She had no friends and killed time by just walking every day until she wore out her shoes and had to put cardboard inside them.

And still she had no word about the fate of her mother and father. She had witnessed unbelievable bloody murder, been driven from her home and country, and lost her parents. It was the lowest point at which a young woman could be. Though she still had hope, at times that hope seemed groundless. The feeling of despair was almost unbearable, and she would cry at night with the lights out, lying in a bunk in a barracks with dozens of other miserable souls.

CHAPTER 4

A New Life

After about three months, Sylvia made contact with some distant cousins who had slipped out of Cuba by boat, and she left the barracks to move in with them. It was hard to live packed in with relatives, but so much better than living in a barracks, and the food had improved. However, she still had no word about her parents. Her relatives were very kind to her and tried to comfort her as best they could under the circumstances.

What Sylvia did not know was that aside from being separated from their daughter, her parents were well, living in a small apartment provided by the state, with just one room and a bathroom down the hall. Alberto's efforts to fool the Revolutionary Guard finally paid off. After being separated from their daughter for so long, they were allowed to leave their homeland to go to Florida to try to find her.

On their arrival in Florida, they were informed by the authorities that Sylvia was living with relatives in Miami. The authorities in Miami were able to bring together the Caballero family after many months of uncertainty. Sylvia was overwhelmed with happiness at being reunited with her mother and father. Now, however, there was work to do. They had to make a new life in another country, and while Sylvia spoke English very well, neither of her parents had a command of the new language. And these industrious folks were not the type to accept welfare.

It was then up to Sylvia to get a job and support the family. She had certain qualities that ensured that she could gain employment—she was smart, had a command of both English and Spanish, and just as important in those days, she was beautiful and charming. So her prospects were very good. However, having good prospects and getting a good job were not the same thing. She wanted a job where she could use her mind and have some responsibility. It took a few weeks, but finally she found one.

The U.S. Navy hired her initially as a clerk, but a navy captain was taken with this young woman who would always come in early and work late. He took her on as his secretary. Soon her job would take a new and important turn that would put Sylvia on a path of responsibility that would become a way of life for her.

THE CUBAN MISSILE CRISIS

Reports from inside Cuba to exiled sources questioned the need for large amounts of ice that were being transported to rural areas. This was relayed to the U.S. government and was enough to prompt U-2 flights over those sections of the island mentioned in the report. These U-2 flights discovered that the Soviet Union had secretly brought into Cuba medium-range ballistic missiles that had the potential to reach every large city in the U.S.

The United States had an arsenal of long-range nuclear weapons much larger than that of the Soviet Union, as well as medium-range ballistic missiles in Turkey, whereas the Soviet Union had a large stockpile of medium-range nuclear weapons located in Europe.

Cuba agreed to accept these missiles, as they were receiving economic aid from the Soviets. The

U.S. then established a quarantine in international waters to stop Soviet ships from bringing in more missiles. This was designated a *quarantine* rather than a *blockade* to avoid issues with international law.

At that time, Sylvia was working for the navy captain (which is the same rank as a full colonel in the army). He asked her to his office.

"Sylvia, what do think of Castro?"

Sylvia said, "He is a murderer and he's a despicable man. I hate him as much as you can hate someone."

"Would you be willing to help us?"

She had no idea how she could help, but said, "Yes, sir. What can I do?"

He gazed at her for some time before saying, "What you would have to do would be something where you could never tell anyone the details of what you learn or know. Would you be prepared to do that?"

Sylvia had already guessed what they wanted her to do—after all, she had worked there during the beginning of the Cuban Missile Crisis and had figured out that she was one of the few bilingual people working around her unit.

She answered, "Yes, sir, you can count on me."

He had the papers all ready for her to sign. After that, for the duration of the crisis, she would spend days and nights listening to the Cubans talking to each other, at all levels, as well as Cubans talking to the Russians.

The Soviets went eyeball to eyeball with President Kennedy, but at the last moment called back their ships. We came very close to World War III. In addition, they agreed to remove the missiles already there in exchange for an agreement that the United States would not invade Cuba. The U.S. also agreed to remove all its missiles from Turkey, though at the time Kennedy did not reveal this concession.

Sylvia was not alone in her work, but the information she relayed to her superiors certainly made a difference and allowed her to play a significant role in one of the most dangerous situations in American history. To this day she has never told me any of the details of what she heard and relayed to her superiors.

Soon, however, Sylvia's keen mind, ability, and her willingness to take on more responsibility would allow her to embark on new challenges.

CHAPTER 5

Puerto Rico

Sylvia's father, Alberto, was a proud and good man, but was out of his element in his new country. His law degree was not worth anything in Miami, and he spoke almost no English. For three years he was restless and unhappy, but his luck was about to change. Sylvia was supporting the family with her job with the navy and she had a good future, but Alberto was a proud Hispanic man and did not like being dependent on his daughter. He was still in good health and still wanted to do work that was in keeping with his education and abilities.

A distant relative of Alberto's, Armando Iduate, an architect, made contact with him and offered him a job as the manager of his architectural firm, Antilles Architecture, in San Juan, Puerto Rico. Because Spanish was the language of this protectorate of the U.S., and her father would have a real job with responsibility, Sylvia agreed to leave her job with the navy and move to Puerto Rico with her parents.

In 1964 the family moved to Puerto Rico. Alberto quickly settled into his new position. He hit it off with Armando, who had his hands full with his profession, and Alberto jumped right in and relieved him of worry about the office and the books. But Sylvia set out to find the best job she could.

She applied for and was hired by the governor's office as a clerk. Again, her hard work, beauty, and personality caught the eye of the governor himself, Roberto Sanchez. Her official title was Governor's Assistant. While she was one of three

Sylvia in evening dress

assistants, she, as usual, was the first one there and the last one to leave. In addition, Sylvia's beauty and personality made everyone around her happy.

Governor Sanchez recognized her special talents and moved her into helping him with his favorite subject: politics. The governor liked to give luncheons and dinners to the members of the Assembly. These were like state senators. The governor was all politics and this was one of the ways he used to get his way with legislation.

Soon Sylvia was heavily involved in planning and hosting these important political functions. For luncheon, she wore regular office clothes, but for evening dinners, he insisted that she wear long evening dresses. While he clearly liked her beauty, he was a gentleman in every respect, and treated

Sylvia on the right, the governor on the left at a political luncheon she organized.

her more like a colleague.

This time was special for Sylvia. Her father was working with the architectural firm and was happy. They had a nice apartment and Sylvia's mother had friends. Sylvia was starting to feel comfortable with her new position of responsibility with the social functions, which allowed Governor Sanchez to work with the Assembly and get his way most of the time.

Sylvia had complete access to the governor and on one occasion went to his office to complain about a newspaper that had printed an article critical of Sanchez. He laughed. "Sylvia, this is nothing. I don't care if they write bad things about me. I just want them to write about me."

The governor, Sylvia, and legislators at the Puerto Rico airport, preparing to fly to Washington, DC.

NOVEMBER 2, 1966

While Sylvia was still in Puerto Rico, a law was passed by Congress and signed by President Johnson putting into place certain protections for Cubans living in the U.S. All Cubans who had entered the U.S. after Castro came to power were legal immigrants. However, that legality was based on an executive order by President Johnson. In theory, any new president could issue another executive order reversing Johnson's order.

To correct this potential problem, on November 2, 1966, Congress passed and Johnson signed into law the Cuban Adjustment Act. The law applied to any native or citizen of Cuba who had been inspected and admitted or paroled into the United States after January 1, 1959, and had been physically present for at least one year. They were now admissible to the United States as a permanent resident.

This was wonderful news, as it meant that all Cubans now in the country did not have to worry about a new executive order returning them to Cuba.

CHAPTER 6

California

Sylvia was very happy working for the governor in Puerto Rico and had no thoughts of moving back to the mainland. However, Alberto had other ideas.

Alberto Caballero was smart and very giving to all around him. He loved his wife and their only child—Sylvia. He had given up the hope that she would become a doctor, but he wanted the best for her and, thinking long term, he believed that to be all she could be she must live in the United States. At that time, the place to find a good future was California.

They had relatives in the Los Angeles and San Francisco areas. Alberto persuaded Sylvia that while giving up her present situation and moving to California would be unnerving, it would be best in the long term. It took courage for such a move into another unknown, but Sylvia's courage was built on the kind of adversity not experienced by most people.

Several days of serious thought went by before Sylvia finally agreed with her father. She informed the governor that she was resigning her position in order to move to the mainland. The governor was upset, as he realized he was losing a valuable assistant who had done a remarkable job of arranging politically based social occasions for the legislators, and he told her so.

Sylvia made the move to San Francisco in early 1967 and quickly gained employment as the assistant to the president of the Coordination Council on Mental Retardation (CCMR). The Council was located on Turk Street and it was not the best part of town. One day, Sylvia left for lunch and a street person asked her for money. She ignored him and was subsequently attacked. She took him down with a kick to his private parts. She was fearless. She had her lunch, and when she returned to her office, the same man was still there. As he saw Sylvia coming, he decided to get lost.

Sylvia was working for the Council when we were married, and the president of the Council would come to dinner at our flat in San Francisco.

She was a really nice person, and a good influence on Sylvia. At our dinners, she raved to me about Sylvia's abilities.

That position was the beginning of Sylvia's future, one that would launch her on a lifetime of service to her fellow man. It stimulated her interest in what was then called mental retardation, and how to help those afflicted with this damning condition.

MARRIAGE

At the time, I was living in San Francisco, having moved there after four years in the navy. I had been hired by a bank, initially as a collector repossessing cars at night (it fit in with my school schedule), and I was working my way through USF, using G.I. loans to pay for my education. After a year, I worked my way up to a loan officer position and was rewarded with an increase in my salary. This meant that I could move out of my studio apartment and into an apartment with a bedroom.

One day, the manager of the branch came to me and asked me to take his secretary, Sue, home as she wasn't feeling well. So I drove her to the apartment she shared with her husband. I was impressed with the location and apartment building, but mentioned to Sue that earlier that morning I had rented an apartment at another place. Sue said that there was a unit available and she suggested that I go back and cancel the deal at the place I had rented. So I did. I returned to the apartment I had just rented, where the manager had not yet cashed the check. I asked her to cancel my rental. She laughed and said, "I knew you would be coming back." She returned my check and I returned to Sue's apartment building and rented the apartment there.

Looking back, it seems to me that if Sue had not become ill and I had not taken her home, I would never have met Sylvia, and my life would have been much different. I have sometimes thought that some marriages are made in heaven, as so many things had to happen in order for Sylvia and I to meet.

I moved in one Saturday in December 1967. It was a furnished apartment, and very nice compared to the last place. That day I went down to the garage to drive to the supermarket for groceries, and parked next to my VW Beetle was a new 1968 red Mustang.

I had stopped to admire the interior, when a young woman said, "Can I get in my car?"

I turned, and there was the most beautiful woman I had ever seen. I apologized for blocking her way and then said, "I'll bet your husband likes your Mustang."

While that was a silly thing to say, she quickly told me, "I don't have a husband."

Then I did something so out of character that I surprised even myself. I asked her for a date.

Sylvia was clearly shocked by my aggressive request and responded, "I don't know you."

I introduced myself—very clumsily, in hindsight.

Sylvia responded, "Nice to meet you, but my parents must approve of anyone I date."

I took this as a nice kiss-off, having received many in the past. But there was something different about her; I wasn't going to give up. "Where are your parents?" I asked.

"They live in Puerto Rico."

I thought I was sunk. But she followed up by saying that her mother was visiting her.

"Take me to your mother," I said forcefully. That was not like me, but it was love at first sight and I wasn't going to let her go until I got a yes about a date.

Sylvia took me to meet her mother, who was a pleasant-looking woman who smiled at me. I asked Sylvia to repeat every word I said to her mother. I began by giving my name and that I worked for a bank. I gave her one of my cards, hoping it would impress her. I asked her for permission to take

Sylvia to the Rosicrucian Egyptian Museum in San Jose the next day (Sunday) and told her I would have Sylvia back by five o'clock. Her mother looked me over from head to toe. After what seemed to be several minutes, she smiled and nodded her approval.

I was ecstatic with happiness and surprised that I had achieved what I'd hoped for. After all, I had never been so insistent when meeting a girl in the past. I was a Southerner who had been taught by my grandmother never to be forward with women. But I was overwhelmed with a joy I had never felt before. I knew at that moment that I had found the woman I wanted to spend the rest of my life with.

We drove down to San Jose the next morning in my little VW Beetle to the Rosicrucian Museum and Planetarium, the largest collection of Egyptian artifacts on exhibit in western North America. I had been to the museum many times, as I was and still am fascinated by ancient Egypt. As it turned out, Sylvia had a similar interest in Egypt.

When we got out of my Beetle, I took her hand. We had a great time at the museum and stayed several hours. But surprise—I did get her home before five o'clock. I never dated another woman after that date with Sylvia, and have devoted my life to her ever since.

On Monday morning, I went to work. Bob Johnson, the manager of the branch, asked how my weekend had gone. I answered that I had met the girl I was going to marry. Bob broke up laughing, saying, "Nolan, I thought you were smart."

He attended our wedding.

For the next six months, Sylvia and I saw each other every day. Why not? We lived in the same building. Besides, I wanted to be with her all the time. I did worry sometimes because I was always at her apartment with her mom. I started to eat most of my meals there. Her mom was a great cook, especially Cuban food.

Since we both had jobs during the week, at night we would go to the movies and occasionally to a café for dinner. But on the weekends, we would take some great trips. We were restricted, however, as Josefina would not allow us to stay overnight. That was all right with us.

When we went to Tahoe, we would get up at three a.m. and take off, getting back at ten or eleven at night having had a wonderful time. Sylvia loved Tahoe, especially the snow. I bought her boots and heavy clothes for the weather and we tried skiing. I found out that Sylvia was very athletic. She quickly became a better skier than I was. On one visit, visitors would take off their shoes and leave them in the shop while they put on ski boots and hit the slopes. We did the same. However, on our return to the shop where we had rented the skis, we found that someone had stolen my shoes, so I had to buy another pair.

What Sylvia loved most about our Tahoe trips were the snowmobiles. In those days, you didn't just go round and round on a track when you rented a snowmobile, like you do today. We had acres of snow-covered country in which to speed around on our rented snowmobiles. And Sylvia loved speed. I was constantly hollering for her to slow down. We would spend hours on those snowmobiles.

Sylvia loved the wine country, too. We made several trips to St. Helena and in Yountville we would stop for lunch. I remember that one of the wineries developed their wines in a mammoth cave and we went in with other folks to see this operation. The man giving the tour said that if anyone stayed too long in that cave, they would get drunk on the fumes. I don't know if the tour guide was just hyping the folks about breathing the fumes, but as we came out, some folks complained about being lightheaded.

Another favorite place was Muir Woods. Being from Cuba, Sylvia was astonished by the size of the 2,000-year-old sequoias. They didn't grow trees like that in Cuba.

We visited Sausalito so often that I started to think how nice it would be to share a houseboat with Sylvia as husband and wife. We could take the ferry to work. I daydreamed that a lot, even though I had not brought up the idea of marriage. Mill Valley was another favorite place to go and wander around in the shops, never buying anything, but it was fun. Fisherman's Wharf was a regular stop, too, with all the tourists, the wax museum, and the fish markets.

We would drive south also. Sylvia liked the Boardwalk in Santa Cruz and we would ride the Giant Dipper—the roller coaster—several times on each visit. In those days the main drag was "hippieville." The counterculture was moving down the coast for the warmer weather and because the tourist buses were cramping their style in the Haight.

We traveled as far south as the Monterey Peninsula, Carmel, and Big Sur. Sylvia loved to be on the go. It wasn't that she was a restless soul, it was her great and curious mind. She wanted to absorb everything around her. She had no limitations as to subjects. I was bombarded with questions about politics, art, sociology, and culture, so I tried to give her my opinion on these subjects as best I could.

Another of her qualities was a sense of humor. She made me laugh continuously. She liked Charlie Chaplin and could walk just like him in *The Little Tramp*.

At the time, I belonged to a club that had a swimming pool. I started taking her as a guest and found out that she was the most graceful swimmer. She would swim with not a ripple and when we would race, I never won. There I was with all my splashing and she just glided ahead of me. I learned that she'd spent lots of time swimming in Cuba. That was it—that satisfied my male ego.

On Sundays I would attend church with her. I wasn't Catholic, nor did I have any religious affiliations, but it made her happy for me to go with her.

About six months later, I asked Sylvia to marry me. She accepted. We went to the church to see about holding the service there, and the priest put me through quite the grilling. I wasn't Catholic and had never been baptized. He asked me why I had never been baptized, and I told him the truth. Neither of my parents were religious in any way. I had not attended any church, other than a brief time at a Baptist church when I was sixteen. The priest was not impressed with this and said that we could not be married in his church.

Sylvia and I were crushed. What were we going to do? Actually, we settled down after a nice lunch and made other arrangements.

On August 31, 1968, we were married in a Lutheran church. I paid the church $75.00 for the service, since that's all the pastor asked for.

It was the beginning of a wonderful life with a woman who would surprise me every day by her sweet nature, superior intellect, creative ability, and strong desire to help everyone, especially children. Looking back, almost everything positive I did in my life was encouraged by Sylvia.

On our honeymoon, we just took off with no destination in mind but driving south. Our first stop was Carmel, where we spent two days. Then we headed south to Big Sur, where we stopped and had lunch at the Nepenthe Inn, an artists' hangout. Eventually we made it to Anaheim and Disneyland. Disney had no rooms available, so we found a nice motel. The man at the desk said they were booked up. The only available room was the honeymoon suite. We took it—it was very large and had a large private swimming pool. We went for a midnight swim just as Disneyland began its nightly fireworks show. What an evening.

The next morning, we went to Disneyland and spent all day there. We rode every ride and the Pirates of the Caribbean three times. We had a late dinner at midnight in a restaurant with a patio, which allowed us to watch the midnight Electric Light parade. We spent two weeks on our honeymoon and then returned to work and living.

Our small apartment was on 20th Avenue, and we wanted something larger. We found a flat on 22nd Avenue owned by a police captain. It was very large, with a formal dining room with French doors and a chandelier, a breakfast nook, and an entrance hall larger than our first apartment. As the police captain was showing the flat, I was thinking there was no way we could afford this place. However, he said we could have it for only $200 a month.

We moved in and to this day I think about living there as a joyful time. We slowly tried to fill our new home with furniture, and without a doubt, the captain was wonderful to us. He would ask if we were happy and what he could do to make it better for us. Actually, he seemed more interested in making Sylvia happy.

The captain invited us to dinner one evening. He lived on the next street over. We met his significant other, a nice lady named Mary who had lived with him for twenty years. She had prepared dinner for us and it was a pleasant evening. At one point, Sylvia was with Mary and I was in the kitchen with the captain. By that time, I felt comfortable talking to him about why he had rented the flat to us so cheaply. I told him that he could have gotten twice the rental that he was charging us. I said, "Don't get me wrong, Captain, we're grateful, and very happy with the flat. But—"

"Come to the bedroom," he said.

In his bedroom he went to a drawer and pulled out a picture, which he showed to me. I was totally shocked. I was looking at Sylvia.

"What? How?" I stammered.

"Nolan, this isn't Sylvia. This is the love of my life. When I was a young man in the navy, I was stationed at the naval base in Cuba, where I met Jannetta. I loved her with all my heart, but the navy wouldn't let us marry. Later, I was transferred out and I was discharged. I went back to Cuba to marry Jannetta, but she wasn't there. I looked for her for months, but never found her. I never stopped loving her and never got married. I've been with Mary for twenty years and I love her, but not the way I loved Jannetta. So when you and Sylvia came to look at the flat, and I saw Sylvia, I cut the price. Just being around her makes me happy. She reminds me of my true love. I hope you and Sylvia live in my flat for a long time. You are a lucky young man, Nolan."

I was totally moved by the captain's confession. He was obviously a good man and meant well, but what was I to do? Move? Tell Sylvia? I covered my predicament well the rest of the evening. After a sleepless night, I decided to say nothing going forward. After all, Sylvia loved the flat and the captain was an honorable man who just wanted us to be happy.

Years later, after we had moved on, I told Sylvia about the captain and his lost love who looked so much like her. She felt very sorry for the captain, as she understood his deep sadness, and she reminded me that those three years on 22nd Avenue were a period of growth and happiness.

CHAPTER 7

Family, Life & School

Sylvia and I did not go back to Atlanta, Georgia, to visit my parents and my other relatives for the first few months of our marriage. The truth is that I dreaded the idea.

First, ever since I had left Georgia after enlisting in the navy, I would only return every three years as a duty trip. I never liked Georgia when I lived there—I disliked the political system, the segregation, the hot summers, and the mosquitoes. My father disliked the same things, but he was wedded to his life and job and family history and would never leave.

Second, while I wasn't worried about my mother and father accepting that I'd married a Hispanic girl, as they were very liberal, I was less sure about some of my other relatives. After all, I hadn't married a southern girl. Besides, on previous visits, a few of my relatives had commented negatively on why in the world I would want to leave Georgia. Some actually complained that I was losing my southern accent. My Uncle Bud, on one of my previous visits, had said I was becoming a Yankee. So I had some legitimate reasons for my concern about taking Sylvia to Georgia.

Sylvia herself was somewhat nervous about the trip. This was partly my fault, as I had jokingly talked about my relatives in North Georgia and had made references to the movie *Deliverance* and about those folks being "gun-toting rednecks." There was some truth to that. At the funeral of my beloved grandfather, who I loved more than anyone in the world, some of the North Georgia relatives showed up in overalls. I was appalled (in hindsight, I was wrong because those were most likely all the clothes they had). I was eighteen, grieving, and thoughtless, so I walked up to some distant cousin and complained that he was not showing the proper respect for my dear Papa. The man looked me in the eye and said, "If you weren't kin, I'd kill you." I knew he meant every word.

Anyway, all of my worried thoughts about our trip to Atlanta did not stop us from going. As it turned out, nothing bad happened. My folks and my relatives (we didn't visit North Georgia) loved Sylvia. My negative feelings were just that—negative feelings. I can't honestly say that I had a good time, nor do I think Sylvia did. But she smiled during the whole visit and charmed everyone with her beautiful smile and caring personality.

*

We lived in San Francisco for a while, but Sylvia did not go to college immediately as planned. Her responsibilities at CCMF were growing and for a while she set aside her desire to return to college. Eventually, though, she left CCMF and enrolled at San Francisco City College.

She had been a 4.0 student for two years at the University of Havana, but it was not possible to get transcripts from Cuba. Sylvia had a 4.0 average at City College, too, and a year after she started junior college, I was offered a better job at First National Bank in San Jose. This was good for Sylvia, as she could enroll at San Jose State University.

In 1971 we moved to Los Gatos. We loved our townhouse. Our landlord was another good man who did everything to make us happy. We had many parties with folks I worked with and Mike Hales (who had been Glen Campbell's lead guitar player before going into banking) would play and sing. Even the landlord and his wife would join in.

Sylvia enrolled at San Jose State. In that same year she became a citizen of our country, which was a very proud moment for us both. This was allowed under the 1966 Cuban Adjustment Act.

On the next page is a photo of her citizenship document.

For the next three years that she attended the university, I never saw her study. She had this ability to absorb the subject in class alone. She graduated with a 4.0 average. Then another shock came.

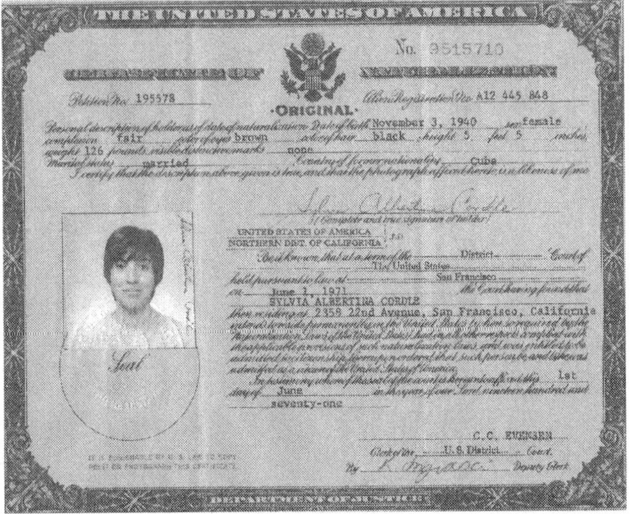
THE UNITED STATES OF AMERICA

No. 9515710

Petition No. 195578

Alien Registration No. A12 445 848

·ORIGINAL·

Date of birth November 3, 1940 sex female

complexion fair color of eyes brown color of hair black height 5 feet 5 inches

weight 126 pounds visible distinctive marks none

Marital status married Country of former nationality Cuba

UNITED STATES OF AMERICA

NORTHERN DIST. OF CALIFORNIA

District Court of The United States

held pursuant to law at San Francisco

on June 1, 1971

SYLVIA ALBERTINA CORDLE

2359 22nd Avenue, San Francisco, California

1st

June

seventy-one

Seal

C.C. EVENSEN

Clerk of the U.S. District Court.

Deputy Clerk

Sylvia was informed that she would not be accepted into the M.S. in clinical psychology program. She was in tears as she called me at my office. Without that two-year Master of Science degree, she could never get her license to work as a school psychologist and a marriage and family counselor. Their reason was that places in those advanced degree programs were reserve for disadvantaged minorities.

I left my office, which was within walking distance of the university, and went to the office of the head of admissions. I walked past the secretary and directly into his office.

"Can I help you, sir?" he said.

"My name is Nolan Cordle, and you will not allow my wife, Sylvia Cordle, who has a 4.0 average, to move on to the M.S. degree. Why not?" I shouted.

The head of the admissions office turned white, but managed to recover enough to invite me to sit down. I continued to stand while he retrieved her file from his file cabinet. He studied it and said, "Yes, she has a 4.0 average, but you must understand, Mr. Cordle, that the university has to follow the government's orders regarding giving minority students preference. After all, it's only fair."

"What kind of university are you running?" I demanded. "Two wrongs don't make a right. And who is considered a minority?" I was so angry I could hardly stop myself from reaching over his desk and doing something I would regret.

"Well, the list includes, of course, blacks and Asian and Hispanics, but others like Pacific Islanders and the like." His explanation seemed to help him regain his composure.

"Does being Cuban qualify as a minority?" I asked with contempt in my voice.

"Sure, but what does this have to do with your wife?"

At this stage, I felt I was not dealing with the brightest light on the block. I snapped, "Because she is Cuban!"

With this, he showed his true feelings about minorities, by stammering, "But she's white." He realized that he had said the wrong thing. "I'm sorry, I didn't mean it that way."

I let him off the hook by saying, "Does she get in?"

"Yes. It's done and I apologize for causing any grief." He walked to his door and closed it. He looked at me and said, "Please, Mr. Cordle, sit down and let me talk in confidence. I personally hate what I have to do, but in order to keep my job, I do what I'm told. I hope someday it will be different and you are right … two wrongs don't make a right. Please don't repeat what I said. You understand?"

I nodded and got up. We shook hands and I returned to my office, where I called Sylvia and gave her the good news.

She attended the two-year M.S. in Clinical Psychology program and graduated with honors.

Next it was on to Sacramento for a battery of tests that lasted several days, which she again easily passed. She was issued the proper certificates and became a School Psychologist and Family Counseling Therapist. She also was credentialed as a Community College Instructor.

This was the beginning of a wonderful career in which she would go on to help hundreds of children and by extension their parents. In other words, she would help thousands of people.

CHAPTER 8

Career

For six months, Sylvia interned at Hope for the Retarded. This was a requirement and she would be evaluated after this period. Working with what were then called "the retarded" was educational, to say the least.

Sylvia liked the organization, but she was critical of the fact that Hope had a mix of retarded and handicapped people, and they did not seem to differentiate between degrees of retardation. She sensed that the handicapped adults and children being treated at Hope seemed to be perpetually embarrassed about being treated as though they were mentally handicapped as well.

She seemed to have an innate understanding that "the system" was failing in dealing with mentally disabled people and the handicapped. That innate ability would, in the coming years, allow her to change the paradigm for treatment everywhere she worked.

The Adult and Child Guidance Center in San Jose had been in operating for over twenty-five years when Sylvia was hired. This organization served the county with therapy for adults, and testing and therapy for children, and in that regard, worked closely with schools and the courts.

Sylvia was the first bilingual therapist hired and she set out to increase the help the Center offered to the Hispanic population. It did not take long before the Center realized just how well she handled her multiple duties of providing therapy to adults and children, and working with schools and the courts.

At that time the ability to test children with learning or behavior problems was still rudimentary. However, Sylvia's innate ability allowed the Center to send her to schools and the courts to assist in solving or helping with certain problems. Soon, she was spending more time in schools and the courts than in the office.

On one occasion, she was called to a school to evaluate a child who had been determined by the teacher to be retarded. He seemed to have no interest in the work assignments and sat motionless in class, saying little to anyone.

Sylvia listened to the teacher and then spent a few minutes with the boy. She then called the mother and asked if she could take her son to the library. With her permission, Sylvia took the boy to the main San Jose library. She followed him as he passed up the section for children and found the science section. In a few minutes he found a book that interested him, and he and Sylvia sat down at one of the tables. He then explained orbital mechanics to Sylvia.

Testing showed that this young boy had an IQ of close to 180. He was placed in a special school for the gifted.

The teacher was upset at her failure to recognize that the boy was just bored with the classroom. His mind was already far beyond what he was getting in his coursework. Sylvia comforted the crying teacher, who meant well, but simply did not have the understanding she needed.

Sylvia began to understand the enormous problems the system had with teachers who, while they might have meant well, nevertheless did not have the education or proper tools to work with children with learning disabilities. This lack of understanding of the complexity of the human mind had led to a "quick fix" mentality. They simply classified any child with learning problems as "retarded," thus condemning those unlucky children to a lifetime of pushing brooms.

Another area in which Sylvia was very effective was with the courts. Judges used her to evaluate criminals who wanted early release from prison, and juvenile offenders subject to hard time.

On one occasion she spent several sessions with a man who had been serving time for molesting children. He wanted early release as, according to him, he was a changed man. In the third session, Sylvia had made him so comfortable that he admitted that he could not wait to visit a few schools after he got out of

Staff Spotlight

Bilingual Skills Enhance Cordle's Effectiveness

Sylvia A. Cordle, MS

Ten years ago, the Adult and Child Guidance Center made a commitment to provide services to all residents of Santa Clara County — in the language of their choice. This was a substantial commitment by an agency which, at the time, provided services in just one language — English.

Spanish-speaking **Sylvia A. Cordle,** MS, staff therapist and credentialed school psychologist, holds a special place in the implementation of that commitment — she was the first bilingual therapist hired by the Center.

prison. Sylvia sent a written report to the judge recommending that the man never be released. The judge agreed.

On other occasions, she would go to juvenile hall to interview delinquent teenagers. Because of her heavy workload, on many occasions these interviews with delinquents, some of whom were violent, would take place after hours. This meant that I got the chance to accompany her to the sessions. I felt a lot of apprehension, as she interviewed these teenagers in rooms that contained only her and the offender. She faced some risk of attack. In fact, on one occasion, the 17-year-old boy did attack her. Fortunately, the guard was quick and the hoodlum was subdued before he could do any damage. Sylvia never had any fear, even after this experience. Perhaps her experiences during the Cuban Revolution gave her this lack of fear.

Long after Sylvia had moved on to new challenges, she still received letters from judges asking her to come back. Sylvia did, in fact, consider being self-employed and working for the courts. However, the insurance costs for protection from lawsuits were prohibitive, and she was not prepared to give up her desire to help children with their problems.

Sylvia was very happy working at the Adult and Child Guidance Center. However, in 1979, I received an offer to head up the retail loan division at First Hawaiian Bank in Honolulu. My salary would triple. We discussed the pros and cons of such a move. After all, she was doing great work for children and I was already a Vice President of First National Bank. We had purchased a little home in the Santa Cruz Mountains, and had no compelling reason to leave our rewarding life for a new life in Hawaii.

First Hawaiian Bank flew us over and gave us the red carpet treatment. With the position came a country club membership, a new Chrysler automobile, and an unlimited expense account for entertaining current and future bank customers. The president wined and dined us for two days and they put us up at the Royal Hawaiian Hotel. Even Sylvia was overwhelmed by the attention. She knew she was employable, and it was finally she who said, "Honey, you can't turn down this opportunity. I can always get a job." To be honest, I was so happy that my wife had agreed and was willing to move on. I wanted the challenge of more responsibility at a larger bank.

CHAPTER 9

Hawaii

Hawaii consists of nine islands and atolls: Oahu, Hawaii, Kauai, Nihau, Maui, Kahoolawe, Moloka'i, Lana'i, Nihoa, and the Kure Atoll. The total population was 1.5 million, mostly on Oahu, where Honolulu is located.

As it turned out, the move to Hawaii was the absolutely right one—especially for Sylvia. She learned more about testing for levels of mental ability than she could ever have learned in California, because Hawaii was twenty years ahead of California in all aspects of testing and in its deeper understanding of what it means to be mentally disabled.

We leased a home in Monolana Heights, a community 1,500 feet up in the Pala mountain range with a view down into the Diamond Crater. A mango tree and several banana trees grew in the yard, and all in all, it was a nice place to live. In the morning I would go out to the deck, pull a mango from the tree, and have a mango milkshake for breakfast.

Our next-door neighbor was a policeman who came over to greet us. He knew all about us already. He said that if we needed anything, to just let him know. It was my first indication that Hawaii was like a small town on the mainland, where everybody knew the business of everyone else.

I started to realize just how powerful the Chairman of the Board of First Hawaiian Bank was when I went to get my new Hawaiian driver's license. I had to pass the written test, which was no problem. But the driver's test was another matter. The lady who was to give me the driver's test did not know I had overheard her saying to a co-worker, "I'm going to fail his *haole* ass."

I went through a minor hell during that driver's test. What saved me was that I was driving my bank car, a new Chrysler. She asked me when I'd bought the car. I said, "It's my bank car."

She quickly said, "What bank do you work for?"

I answered, "I work for Johnny Bellinger at First Hawaiian Bank."

The lady got all nervous and said, "You passed, sir. I'm sorry, please don't be mad at me. Please don't tell Mr. Bellinger that I gave you a rough time." She began to whimper.

This woman, who had declared she was going to fail me because I was white, was now so frightened of Bellinger that she was reduced to pleading. I got my driver's license. I also assured the poor woman that she was safe from harm. This would not be the last situation where I would be reminded of how these islands were governed by a powerful ruling class.

I learned over time that, with few exceptions, the government was run by the Japanese, the land and businesses were owned by the Chinese, and white folks were brought over from the mainland to run certain businesses or to give certain expertise to those businesses. I was there because I had knowledge the bank needed.

Native Hawaiians, Samoans, and other Islanders were doing manual labor type work. As long as I could do my job and keep the bank happy, they would make sure that Sylvia and I had comforts and things that would make our life easy.

As an example, when we traveled away from Hawaii and returned, we did not have to go through any check-in or questions at the airport. Our bags were gifts from Bellinger and they had the First Hawaiian Bank ensign in plain view. They just waved us through. When we traveled within the islands, we would take the bank's Lear jet. Bellinger insisted that Sylvia and I fly first class, always, when I had to fly to the mainland for bank business.

Sylvia's first position was with the Kapiolani Children's Medical Center as a staff psychologist. She only worked there for about nine months, before moving on to the State of Hawaii's Department of Education, but she did some important work.

On one occasion, a teenage girl was brought to the hospital, having slit both wrists in an attempt to kill herself. Sylvia spent several sessions with her over a few months and got her back to a more stable condition. Two years later, after Sylvia had moved on to the Department of Education, we got an invitation to attend the young girl's graduation from high school. We attended the outdoor ceremony and Sylvia got a pleasant surprise.

The valedictorian was the same young teenager to whom she had given therapy sessions. The young lady gave a rousing speech about going out and facing the challenges of the future and she terminated her speech by thanking a few folks. She smiled and said, "I'd like to thank three people for where I am today … my dear mother and father for putting up with me, and Sylvia Cordle, sitting in the third row. Without her guidance, I wouldn't be standing here today."

As tears ran down Sylvia's cheeks, I was so proud of her, as I had been and would be many, many more times.

In 1980, Sylvia was hired by the Department of Education and her immediate boss was Fran Jorgensen. Fran had been born and raised in Hawaii. In fact, her father was a doctor who had spent most of his career in the Kalaupapa Leprosy Colony on the Island of Moloka'i. Fran had grown up in the Colony.

The Colony was founded in 1865 by King Kamehameha V to "act to prevent the spread of Leprosy" on the remote Kalaupapa Peninsula. Father Damian, a Belgian priest, ran the Colony until his death in 1889, when he succumbed to the disease. It is unknown how leprosy was introduced to Hawaii, but it quickly took a toll on the population, especially among the native Hawaiians, who had no immunity to foreign diseases. In 1969 the state stopped admitting patients to the Colony and a maximum of only 100 visitors were admitted each day, including state and federal workers.

Leprosy (Hanson's Disease) was and still is a problem in Hawaii, but most mainlanders don't know it. Fran wanted to serve the children living in the Colony, but most of the school psychologists working for her wanted no part of going to that place.

Fran was a very talented person and an excellent manager. Sylvia immediately impressed her. As usual, Sylvia was the first one to work and the last to leave. She spent many hours on the weekend studying the different tests used by the staff. Hawaii was twenty years ahead of California in testing, because they understood that there were different levels of mental disability. By learning all the tests to determine the age equivalence of a mentally disabled person, would it be possible to put him or her in a classroom at their age equivalency and be able to teach them basic writing and reading skills? For the first time, Sylvia had the tools to help her do what she innately understood—to help people with different levels of disability. Something that California didn't seem to understand.

Because of our move to Hawaii, Sylvia had benefited more than she could then know. Her familiarity with these tests would allow her to do wonderful things for the rest of her productive life.

One night, Fran came to our home for dinner. We discussed many subjects. Fran complained that her school psychologists were reluctant to go to the Leprosy Colony for fear of catching the dreaded disease.

Sylvia spoke up. "I'll go, Fran, any time you need me to go."

I didn't say a word. Frankly, the thought of Sylvia going to a leper colony frightened me, but I wasn't about to object. I had learned that Sylvia was a strong-willed person and when she wanted to go in a certain direction, she was usually right, and it was best for me to support her.

Sylvia made dozens of visits to the Colony. Despite its being closed to further admissions in 1969, due to recent developments in antibiotics to control the disease, there were still several hundred patients living there, including dozens of children.

One day, I was having lunch with Johnny Bellinger, the chairman of the board at the bank. He said, "I hear Sylvia is testing in the Colony ... you know, Nolan, you are a lucky man. Sylvia has more balls than most of my executives, and she is the only wife that does important work. Hang on to her."

I asked him how he knew about Sylvia's visits to the Colony. He smiled and said, "Everybody knows. Hawaii is a small place."

The bank had a 55-acre retreat on Oahu for the senior executives to use on their time off. It contained twenty small A-frame houses for each senior executive and their families, a swimming pool, tennis courts, and walking paths. It was, in short, a luxurious resort.

Bellinger wanted all the senior executives and their families to meet once a month for a weekend together. He provided entertainment in the evening with roving Hawaiian groups in the long house. So we gathered.

On one particular Saturday night, Bellinger, his wife, and all the other senior executives and their wives were in the long house, sitting in a circle making general conversation. All the wives were wearing long dresses called muu-muus. All except Sylvia, who was wearing black pants, black high heels, and a beautiful green and black Hawaiian shirt. She looked stunning.

One of the wives said, "Sylvia, why don't you wear a muu-muu? All of us wives always wear them."

Sylvia said, "Well, to be honest, I don't particularly like them." Everyone fell silent. The women got a look on their faces that seemed to say, *Now you're in trouble.*

But Bellinger smiled and said, "Sylvia, I like muu-muus, but I admire your honesty. You have more balls than most of the men who work for me." He laughed as a signal that everyone had better appreciate what he'd just said. Everyone gave a nervous laugh ... and suddenly, Sylvia was popular with everyone.

For six years we had a great life in Honolulu. Sylvia continued to do great work. In that period, she tested and set up programs for hundreds of children. I was getting more responsibility, too. Our weekends were filled with people.

We became friends with Arthur and Catherine Murray, who had become famous in the fifties with their dance studios and TV show. They had millions in First Hawaiian and I was assigned to keep them happy. Actually, Sylvia and I enjoyed the association.

I had mentioned to Sylvia that Arthur and Catherine were famous, but being from Cuba, she had never heard of them. One night we were watching *The Merv Griffin Show*, and when his first guests came out, Sylvia was almost in shock. "That—that's Arthur and Catherine," she shouted.

Catherine was always praising Sylvia for her looks. While having dinner one night, she said to her, "My dear, did you ever do any acting?"

Sylvia answered, "No."

"Well, you should." Catherine said. "You are so beautiful."

Arthur and I both nodded our agreement.

Because of my work, Sylvia and I associated with a few very famous people. Frankly, Sylvia navigated this territory better than I did. She had natural charm, which grabbed the attention of these folks. Whenever I was at a loss for words, she could get the conversation going by asking questions. She was absolutely at ease with the rich and powerful.

General Frederick C. Weyand (1916–2010) was a senior vice president at the bank. He had been a four-star general, head of the Joint Chiefs of Staff, and the commander of the II Field Force in the Vietnam conflict. We had become friends because together, we did most of the speeches to groups about the bank and other economic matters. Bellinger, the chairman, and Walter Dodds, the president and my boss, did not like to give speeches.

At dinner one night, the general excused himself to go to the restroom. Sylvia asked Mrs. Weyand why he, who could have had any job in Washington, would come to work at a bank in Hawaii. It was a very bright and relevant question, but one that I would not have had the guts to ask.

"Well, Sylvia," she replied, "I didn't want any more to do with Washington, the politics and all … so I told Fred that if we didn't go as far away from there as we could, I was going to divorce him. Fred knew I meant it … so here we are."

I could not have asked such a personal question, but Sylvia pulled it off, apparently with no offense to Mrs. Weyand.

Alexander Haig was Secretary of State at the time and he was on his way to Japan. At one time he was in charge of NATO, so he decided to stop in Hawaii and visit his old boss, General Weyand.

I got a call from the general. "Nolan, come to my office." I hurried to his office to find the chairman, the president, and several other senior officers … and Secretary of State Haig. I was introduced to the Secretary. We all stood around feeling important, while Secretary Haig spoke about his responsibilities.

That night the general and I had to give speeches to a group at a hotel. As we drove, I said, "It was nice meeting Secretary Haig. He seems like a nice and smart man."

The general laughed and said, "Nolan, he's a dumb shit. But you're right, he is a nice man. Yes, he did everything I told him to do at NATO. I didn't want a thinker in that position, only someone who would do what I told him."

I discussed this and other things that the general volunteered to me about the president and other powerful people. Sylvia understood that the powerful were human beings, too. Some were good and some were bad and some were in between. But she, as I have said, was at ease with everyone. She showed no fear of Bellinger, General Weyand, or any other person.

Dr. Thomas Hitch was President Johnson's economic advisor and was well known when Bellinger gave him one full floor of the bank's main headquarters. Hitch set up the best economics library in Hawaii. Bellinger gave him a huge salary, the title of senior vice president, and put him in a position of great influence over the economic reality of Hawaii. Dr. Hitch was by all accounts a good man and a brilliant economist, no doubt, but he did carry a degree of arrogance in any conversation with anyone, except with Sylvia.

We had dinner at his home many times and I would just sit at the table listening to Sylvia and Dr. Hitch go on for hours about life and philosophy. He wanted her to talk about Cuba and the economic problems caused by Castro. Sylvia obliged by telling him some of the problems she had seen for three years under Castro. Because of his liking for Sylvia, he was always willing for his staff to supply me with any economic data I needed.

Sylvia actually had the ability to represent the bank, and in fact, I was able to make some great deals for the bank that would not have been possible without her.

As one example, I rented a very large room at a nice hotel and threw a party for every auto dealership on the Island. A new dealer was invited. As he walked in, he said to me, "Mr. Cordle, I stopped by just for a minute to pay my respects … as you know, I've gone with another bank."

"That's okay, come on in," I said.

Sylvia asked him what was he was drinking and brought him his drink. She spent a few minutes with him and later came back to converse with him.

This man, who had said he didn't want to do business with my bank, and was only going to stay at the party for a few minutes, was the last person to leave. He said to me, "Walk me back to my room."

As we walked, he started raving about Sylvia. She had apparently sold him on both me and First Hawaiian. "You can have my business," he said. That was nine million dollars in flooring loans and large bank accounts and first pick at financing all his auto loan requirements.

I later asked Sylvia how she'd pulled it off. "Oh, I just told him how much I loved my husband, because you were the most honest person I have ever known. He asked me where I was from and I told him … and about coming to America for a better life. He talked about his wife. She died of cancer and he missed her very much. I just listened to him."

On a customer's yacht, Hawaii

Some of the bank's customers were so enamored with Sylvia that they would show it in dynamic ways.

Take Carl Oberocker, owner of the BMW Agency. He also owned the Rolls Royce and Jaguar dealerships. He was German and was a brilliant man, who had great respect and affection for Sylvia.

One Saturday he called our home and wanted Sylvia and me to accompany him to the airport to pick up the new manager of his service department. According to Carl, his new manager was the best service manager in Germany, and he had been lucky to get him to come to Hawaii.

Carl, Sylvia, and I picked up the new manager at the airport and after introductions, Carl invited all of us for lunch at the Hilton Hotel. We sat outside with a nice view of the beach and ocean. The new manager was very talkative and started talking about all the problems that the U.S. had in Miami, with the infusion of "all those Cubans bringing crime to the city." Apparently, this man hadn't understood that Sylvia was Cuban.

Suddenly, Carl snapped, "What are you saying? Sylvia is Cuban. How dare you talk like this in front of her? You sonofabitch, you're fired. Go back to Stuttgart." Carl turned to Sylvia and me and said, "Let's go."

We had not even ordered, so we left the man sitting there in shock. As we walked to Carl's car, Sylvia said, "Carl, it's okay. Don't fire the man."

Carl answered, "Nobody insults my friends—especially you, Sylvia."

Sylvia was amazing in how she could jump between helping me with my challenges at getting business at the bank and working at mastery of a dozen different tests to determine the age equivalence of mentally disabled individuals.

Many times, she would have to go to homes. On one occasion, she went to a home to test a child and knocked on the door, with no answer. The front door was open, but the screen door was closed. She could see into the living room and no one was in sight. She thought that everyone might be in the backyard, so she walked around to the back only to find rows of marijuana plants. She left quickly, as she knew that many people had been shot for walking into such a location. Hawaii was famous for its marijuana crop.

CHAPTER 10

Back to California

About a year after Sylvia and I were married, her father and mother moved to San Francisco. Alberto was getting older and had made enough money to live comfortably. They lived about a mile from our flat on 22nd Avenue. We got together often at Sylvia's parents' place, where Josefina would make Cuban dinners and afterward Alberto and I would play dominoes at the kitchen table.

After we moved to Hawaii, we invited them to come over to visit us. Our intention was to get them to move in with us, as we had a house large enough to accommodate them, because they were getting old and we wanted to look after them.

They did come over and stayed two weeks. Alberto hated Hawaii, especially Honolulu. He missed San Francisco, as he had a few Spanish-speaking friends there, and he knew the city and how to get around in it. He refused to have any discussion about moving to Hawaii and living with us.

So, to help with keeping an eye on her parents, we would fly to San Francisco on the weekends every chance we got. It wasn't a perfect solution, but it was all we could do.

We were aware that Alberto had a problem, mostly from a lifetime of smoking cigars. His shortness of breath was noticeable. Finally, it became clear that we were going to have to return to California. Family comes first, always. We handed in our resignations and hopped on a plane.

We had never sold our home in Los Gatos, so we returned there as a base, but stayed a lot with her parents in their flat, sixty miles north in San Francisco. Alberto died about a year later. He suffered a great deal during that time.

Sylvia with her parents, Josefina and Alberto.

Sylvia returned to her old position with the Adult and Child Guidance Center, where they were happy to have her back, and I started my own consulting firm.

We both missed the rewarding careers we'd had in Hawaii, but we were healthy, and doing well otherwise. So we got on with our lives. Sylvia continued to do wonders for Adult and Child Guidance, while I was on the road a lot, traveling to many states helping banks to solve their problems.

When the Loma Prieta earthquake struck in 1989, it was a tough time for everyone. When it hit at 5:04 p.m., I was on my way back from Sacramento, where I had been doing some consultant work. Sylvia was in her office. There were no cell phones in those days, so I drove to Sylvia's office, but it was closed. Sylvia, as usual, was thinking of her co-workers and was running some of them to their homes. I made it home before they closed Highway 17. Fortunately, unlike many, many others, our home was still intact, with no real damage. I was anxious to see Sylvia, but given her survival ability, I felt sure she was all right.

By the time Sylvia took some of her fellow staff members home, the county had closed Highway 17. She had to find another way home. It took her two hours via the back roads off Highway 9, dodging big rocks, which were all over the roads, landslides, and crevasses. But finally, she was in my arms.

For six months, our community outside Los Gatos had no water. We showered at a club in Los Gatos. Sylvia went back to work immediately.

She contacted the county and offered to give counseling sessions to anyone in need of help with the trauma of the earthquake. The county set up a location for her and advertised the free help. Sylvia spent every weekend for several weeks, eight hours a day, helping folks cope with their trauma. Almost all of the people she helped were women. Sylvia suggested that men might be too embarrassed, and that their egos would not allow them to accept help.

The county gave her a Recognition Award for "outstanding and valuable service to the community." As usual, Sylvia just moved on. She seemed to have no interest in acknowledging to herself that she'd done a wonderful thing for the people of our damaged communities. Her personality was just so giving. It was as if it were in her genes.

*

By 1990, Sylvia wanted to work only with children. She applied for a position as School Psychologist with the Monterey County Office of Education (MCOE) and was hired.

Sylvia would have to drive 55 miles every day to their location in Salinas, then 55 miles back after work. Also, she would be assigned to schools all over Monterey County. This was a daunting challenge, but her desire to serve children was great and she was prepared to do the driving.

She joined a large team of school psychologists serving Monterey County. They were all nice people, but Sylvia was appalled by the status quo there. There was not one in that group of serious individuals with the understanding that there were different degrees of mental disability, and they knew nothing about testing to find out the mental age level of an individual with such a condition. While she was talking to one of her peers about this, he closed his remarks by saying, "After all, they are just retarded." Sylvia was shocked by his seeming lack of knowledge—to say nothing of his lack of professionalism.

After working in Hawaii and with the Adult and Child Guidance Center, she had a moment of regret at having made this move. How was she going to fit in? It would be easy to just fall into line, to get along with everyone and simply draw her salary. However, that would not be Sylvia. She was going to do it her way—the right way.

After she received her assignments to schools all over Monterey County, in locations like King City and Fort Hunter-Liggett, Sylvia made an appointment with the administrator who had given her the position, the Superintendent of Schools. Sylvia had to be very careful if she was going to suggest that MCOE could improve the way they tried to help their constituents. She did not want to imply to the superintendent that his staff needed to re-educate themselves both in their knowledge of testing and in their understanding that these children were not "just retarded."

The superintendent listened intently and then said, "Sylvia, why do you think I hired you? Remember, you told me your philosophy and your knowledge of testing. I'm new myself, and was as disappointed as you at the way this place operates. But with your knowledge and help, we can change things."

I personally spoke in private to the superintendent at a social function. He made it clear to me that he thought Sylvia was an incredible talent, and he was depending on her to lead the charge to change the paradigm of treatment in his district.

I was so proud of Sylvia; she had committed to changing a whole system. An enormous challenge.

CHAPTER 11

One Person

Over the next 16 years, Sylvia, with the backing of the superintendent, did wonderful things for the children of Monterey County. Eventually, she completely changed the ineffective system to one that could actually help them.

The school psychologists in the system, while well-intentioned people individually, had become so comfortable with an inadequate system that at times they fought Sylvia with the same antiquated argument: The children they served were "just retarded." Merely identifying the individual as retarded meant they were doing their jobs. They seemed not to have the slightest interest in improving their effectiveness. They were comfortable with working eight hours a day and drawing their very nice salaries. But Sylvia never complained about any of them being lazy or inadequate, only that they didn't understand.

She would come home after a ten- or twelve-hour day exhausted. I constantly worried about the 55 miles of highway that she had to navigate at night to make it home safely. I'm sure that in her heart, she had some negative feelings about some of her co-workers, as we all do, but her personality would not allow negative talk to get in the way of her mission. She believed that by continuing to test, and with seeing the positive results of those tests, her fellow school psychologists would come around and start asking her to show them how to use them.

Regardless of the lack of progress she made with the staff, she still had her rounds to make all over Monterey County. From large schools to some with only one room, she had to win over teachers and principals if she was going to be as successful as the superintendent wanted. It became evident to her that winning over the schools would help her stand the best chance of changing the paradigm. Sylvia stopped bringing up the subject of testing with her fellow staff members. Instead, she developed friendly relationships with everyone.

Many times it was necessary to work on the weekends. She would have to go into homes in remote places to test kids who could hardly speak English. Many times, when I could, I would accompany her to the homes of these children being tested. What I saw left an indelible impression on me.

Only seventy miles from Silicon Valley, where cutting-edge technology was being invented daily, Sylvia and I would go into homes that had dirt floors, whose occupants were field workers from across the border. Mostly, the parents of the children she was testing could speak little English, and Sylvia's bilingual talents came in handy. Another serious problem that she had to deal with initially was how few attempts there had been made to teach English to the children of immigrants from Mexico.

Sylvia began to talk up the idea to the principals of the schools that unless these children could master English, they could not be all they could be. This was not fair to these children, many of whom had been born in this country and were U.S. citizens.

Slowly, Sylvia got the point across to the schools that no school psychologist could tell very well between behavior that was the result of mental disability or simply a learning disability. She was the master of half a dozen cutting-edge tests to distinguish between the two.

Over the years, her belief in the necessity of teaching English caught on with the principals and teachers. In fact, whenever possible, teaching English to the children of immigrants is now an established policy. And Sylvia played a major role in the eventual establishment of that policy.

One reason that she was eventually able to change the system for the better, was that she was the only bilingual school psychologist. It is hard to believe that, given the fact that so many children in Monterey County were Hispanic, the administration did not consider hiring bilingual school psychologists a necessity.

Almost every week, Sylvia had to spend Saturday or Sunday visiting homes in order to test children. Her workload was heavy, but was made more so by her insistence on completing any challenge one hundred percent. She had such a love for these disadvantaged children that she was, in a word, driven.

One Sunday, I accompanied her to Fort Hunter-Liggett to test a little boy having problems with his attention span. The Fort was very large, about 200,000 acres. On the property is the Mission San Antonio de Padua, established in 1771. We planned to attend services, which were at nine a.m. every Sunday, so we left home very early, as the Fort was 95 miles away.

After being admitted at the gate, we drove to a crossroad, where we had to turn right. I turned right and saw we were behind a tank. I looked in the rear view mirror and saw another tank. We were in a convoy of tanks on maneuvers, an unnerving position to be in. Soon, an M.P. on a motorcycle drove up beside our car and shouted at us to take the next turn. He was obviously worried about our safety.

We finally made it just in time to attend church. Later, we visited the 12-year-old boy. His father was an officer in the army, and he and his wife were very worried about their son's problem.

Sylvia spent three hours with the boy, using various tests. The examination revealed that he had a normal intellect, but had serious dyslexia. Over the next few weeks, she developed a program to override the condition and the boy began to do normal work in school. His parents sent Sylvia a thank-you letter.

As the months went by, Sylvia continued to work long hours. Since she was the only bilingual school psychologist, the MCOE used her to work with the Hispanic children, which meant that eighty percent of the time, she had to deal with the toughest problems in the county—children who, through no fault of their own, were trying to survive in a system they didn't understand.

In many cases, the children suffered from emotional problems related to their poor academic performance. Almost always, these problems originated with the parents—fathers who had no real education and who worked hard in the fields. However, some fathers would turn to alcohol or drugs as a solution to their unhappiness. A mother might work as hard as mothers do, with little or no English, five children, a house with dirt floors and no running hot water, limited money to buy food, and a husband who would come home drunk and beat her and the children.

Some of the scenes witnessed by Sylvia on entering some of migrant laborers' homes cannot be written down. They are just too graphic and I don't have the writing skills to commit them to paper. Needless to say, they involved sex between siblings. While Sylvia truly was dedicated to her profession, some of these instances would shake up her normal solid composure. By law, she was required to tell the authorities of domestic abuses, which put her in some danger of retribution.

In some cases, she had success in getting families to understand that their behavior was contributing to their child's problems at school. But more often than not, she could not change the behaviors of a lifetime in uneducated migrant workers with feelings of inferiority.

For my part, I was amazed at the multiple problems Sylvia had to manage. Not only with testing, but working with her peers, with already established ways that were ineffective, with teachers, students, parents ... and, where it was necessary, giving therapy to children and/or their parents. And the miles she had to drive—she wore out three Jeeps during that 16-year period.

Occasionally, she had to help a child whose parents were wealthy and white. In some ways this was more difficult than working with the children of migrant workers.

Well-educated, wealthy white parents sometimes had a difficult time accepting the possibility that their little boy or girl could have any learning difficulties or even a low IQ. After all, didn't their child have their good genes? It must be the teacher's fault. Some of these parents resented a Hispanic woman testing their child, and on more than one occasion they would ask for a non-Hispanic to work with their child. They felt so sure of their superiority that they saw nothing wrong with this position. Sylvia took these rejections by bigoted folks in her stride.

In all fairness, some had no such racist attitudes. They appreciated a good school psychologist whatever his or her race or ethnicity, and would accept with gratitude Sylvia's help with their children. She received many letters of thanks.

Sylvia's success rate was gaining notice by teachers and her peers. The superintendent was very pleased also, and that was the most important thing. He helped keep the wolves at bay. The wolves were almost everyone at first. Human nature being what it is, when we are comfortable with the way things are, why change? But as the months and years went by, one by one the snarling wolves began, either by inclination or survival instinct, to come around to asking Sylvia to show them how to test. Sylvia was obliging, but at the same time, she had a busy schedule and could only devote a limited amount of time to instructing others on the use of these very helpful testing units.

Those who changed and learned new ways became more effective. Many of these wolves would mellow and some became dear friends to Sylvia. Many of her new friends would make the long drive up to our home to have dinner with us, or we would go down south to visit them.

Sylvia had, as they say, been accepted at MCOE. It took five or six years, but it was worth the effort. Sylvia, like all productive people, wanted to be appreciated for her efforts and liked by the people around her. She wanted to accomplish her goals in life and have friends at work. She had achieved both, and was most happy and contented for the remainder of her time at MCOE.

Every year at Christmas, we would go out and buy gifts for every child she was working with at the time. She would take a list and pick out a unique gift for a particular child based on her knowledge of his or her personality. She would wrap each gift and attach a message. She would spend a thousand dollars or more each Christmas, and we would deliver each gift to each child's home on the weekend. It was exhausting, but it made her happy, so I was delighted to help her. I witnessed the joy that disadvantaged children and their parents had at receiving even a small toy at Christmas.

None of her friends ever knew she was giving the children gifts at Christmas, because she never made a big deal out of it. It was just Sylvia—the most giving person I have ever known. We never had children of our own. But Sylvia had hundreds, and she looked at each one with all the love a woman could give her own children. And these children loved her, too. Children seem to know, don't they?

Children seem to go to her like metal to a magnet. Many times at supermarkets, we would be in the vegetable section and children would leave their mother, come to her, and reach out to touch her hand. Mothers would react in two different ways to their children's leaving them to go to a stranger. Some would smile and come over to say hello. Others were more protective and would demand that their child return to them.

One woman wanted to know about Sylvia—who was this woman for whom her daughter would leave her? What did she do for a living?

I spoke up and said that Sylvia was a school psychologist.

The lady said, "That explains it."

To a degree, the woman was right.

CHAPTER 12

Voyages of Discovery

Sylvia's idea of a vacation was not simply taking a cruise or lying on a beach with a book. To her, a vacation was a time of discovery. She had a strong desire to visit all of Western Europe. Perhaps she had some feeling for her roots in Europe, as her grandparents had been Basque from northern Spain. Her mother was a Bilbao, the name of the

On the balcony at the Plaza Athenee, Paris.

major city in northern Spain. However, the more likely reason was her constant desire for discovery. She would talk about visiting London, Paris, and Venice, and of visiting the great museums such as the Louvre in Paris.

Our first destination, then, was Paris, where we took a suite at the Plaza Athenée. What a beautiful hotel! Many of the people staying there brought their dogs, because in France, dogs are treated like humans and allowed in hotels and restaurants. Sylvia and I both liked that, as we loved our dog and often wished that we could take him into restaurants in the U.S. Anyway, that evening we dined at one of the two restaurants owned by the hotel, the Relais Plaza, located on a side street around the corner. I called the desk and made reservations, and the clerk said someone would come and escort us to the restaurant. We thought that was odd. Was it safe on the streets at night?

Thaxton and Sylvia at the Relais.

Actually, safety wasn't the issue. It was convenience. The hotel had an underground passageway that led to the restaurant and a staff member took us through to the most beautiful restaurant we had ever seen. The restaurant had opened for business in 1936 and was decorated in the Art Nouveau style. And since we were staying at the hotel, we got a choice table. The service was impeccable and the food was wonderful, too.

The very next day, Sylvia wanted to go to the Louvre, which was established in 1792, and has an incredible 2,260,420 square feet of floor space.

We spent six hours in the most incredible museum we had ever been in. From the *Winged Victory of Samothrace*, a second-century marble sculpture of the goddess Nike, to the *Mona Lisa*, the 1517 painting by Leonardo da Vinci of Lisa del Giocondo, to *Venus de Milo*, the 100 BC statue, to great painters like Rembrandt, to Egyptian antiquities from the Pharaonic period—the list went on and on. It was an amazing experience and Sylvia insisted on going back again before we left Paris.

We did return the next day, but we separated for an hour so that I could study the works of Rembrandt. Sylvia continued her tour.

I learned a lot by studying his works of art from a distance. I learned that he used the color black. Black isn't a color and many artists today will not use black in their paintings. I have personally been admonished by a peer for using black in my paintings. But if Rembrandt used black, I think I'll continue to do the same. These priceless works of art were roped off and every time I got up from the bench and came close to the ropes to get a better look, a guard would approach and motion to me to back off.

The Louvre was originally a fortress built by the French king Philippe Auguste, who ordered it built in 1190 to protect Paris. In the basement you can walk around the original walls and view the piers that supported the drawbridge.

We spent the next few days visiting all the things that make Paris one of the greatest cities in all the world. We took a boat trip down the river Seine, which flows right through the heart of Paris.

It was and still is the major avenue for commerce and transportation for the city. This is a great way to get a first glimpse of many of the major attractions of the City of Light. Even the dozens of bridges that cross the

Seine are works of art. Many of the structures we read about are visible from the river—the Eiffel Tower, Notre Dame, and the Musée d'Orsay, probably the best museum in the world if you favor Impressionistic art.

Sylvia loved the d'Orsay, as Impressionism is her favorite. In 1900, it was a railroad station and was later converted into a beautiful museum.

We visited the usual things that folks visiting Paris want to see—the Eiffel Tower, the Arc de Triomphe, the Madeline Church, and the Avenue des Champs Elysées. One of the places where Sylvia wanted to spend some time was the Sorbonne University, founded in 1257. While attending the University of Havana, she had dreamed of one day going to the Sorbonne. We spent several hours at the university.

Sylvia was captivated by Notre Dame, but we both

were even more impressed by a smaller church, St. Germain des Pres, which was built fifty years before Notre Dame. It is still an active church and was the church where the Crusaders would stop for services on their way to liberate Jerusalem. Sylvia and I sat taking in the history. She would touch the walls and talk about how the Crusaders would have touched the same walls. We just sat quietly in the church for about an hour. There was something wonderful about being in this historical place where the spirits of the Crusaders prayed that we did not feel at Notre Dame.

ST. GERMAIN

We took a trip to Versailles—both the city and the palace. The town of Versailles is a wealthy suburb of Paris, some 12 miles southwest of the capital. Versailles looks "rich" everywhere you look. We had dinner that evening at a beautiful restaurant and took a late train back to Paris.

The palace was begun by Louis XIII in 1623 as a hunting lodge in brick and stone, and was enlarged into a royal palace by Louis XIV and finally finished in 1710. To say that this palace is opulent doesn't do it justice. The Hall of Mirrors, the Queen's bedchamber in the grand apartments, the Galerie des Bataies, the Chapel, the Opera and marble court—the whole palace is overwhelming to the senses, and not in a totally positive way. It was somewhat offensive to Sylvia's feelings toward the larger part of humanity. But still, it was worth the trip. The Palace is still used for political functions, and the French Parliament meets there in special sessions from time to time.

Versailles

Some of the wonderful places Sylvia wanted to go included Switzerland, Southern France, the wine country of Bordeaux, Dijon, and Strasbourg. Dijon was a smaller version of Paris. We stayed at a hotel that was 500 years old and visited Cathedrale Saint-Benigne, built in 1280, and its underground tombs, which date from 1026.

Strasbourg is one of the truly beautiful cities in France. It was once part of Germany and parts of it are the same as they were 800 years ago.

Then we moved on to Austria—Salzburg, Durnstein, Innsbruck, and Vienna. Salzburg, of *The Sound of Music* fame, is very beautiful—but to its residents, it is famous only as the birthplace of Mozart. We attended services in the cathedral where "Maria" was married. It lasted two and a half hours and we had to stand due to the number of people there.

In Dernstein, we had lunch on the Danube. On the other side were acres of wine grapes, and the boats drifted by. The service and ambiance were something that we always remembered, more than visiting the Cathedral in Salzburg. Sylvia and I have talked many times about how strangely the mind works. We travel great distances to see famous and great things, but still, sometimes it's the little moments like lunch in Dernstein that we cherish.

SALZBURG, AUSTRIA

Innsbruck was a beautiful old city that in the winter is a

leading ski resort. When I drove up to the hotel, a young man greeted us and carried our luggage up to our room. The hotel had a nice restaurant so we went down to eat late in the evening, after we'd seen the old town.

Sylvia never misses a thing. She said to the young man waiting on us, "Do you have a twin?"

He spoke very good English and said, "No, miss, I'm the one who took your luggage up to your room."

Sylvia said, "How many hours do you work?"

"I work fifteen hours a day, six days a week until winter, and then I just ski. I don't work. Someday I want to go to the Olympics." He was so taken with Sylvia that every few minutes he would come to our table and ask if she needed anything.

INNSBRUCK, AUSTRIA

Vienna is a big city. When you drive there, you must park outside of the perimeter of the main part of the city, which is encircled by a road. You can then ride the bus or take a taxi into town. There is a lot to see in this capital city of Austria, but for some reason, Sylvia and I did not ever have sweet memories of it.

As we drove through Germany on the Autobahn, Sylvia saw a sign that read DACHAU. She insisted on going to this infamous "final solution" camp. I had misgivings because I'm a history buff and knew what this was all about. We had discussed it together. Anyway, as usual, I go where my soul mate wants to go.

Dachau concentration camp was the first of its kind established in Germany by the Nazi government in 1933, and it served as a model for later concentration camps. It was designed to hold Jews, political prisoners, and other "undesirables."

THE OVENS AT DACHAU, GERMANY

It was all I expected it to be and more. From the moment we entered the gate, a depressed and somber mood came over us and all around us. When we walked to the gas chambers, Sylvia started to cry. She tried to speak softly, but her voice was trembling as she said, "Oh, God … what I went through was nothing—nothing." I hugged her and tried to comfort her as best I could, but I was close to tears myself. How could a people, the most educated in Europe, allow this to happen? Six million souls died for no reason but their faith. Later, after we returned home, Sylvia pointed out to me that the Jews had done more for their fellow man than anyone—from Nobel Peace Prizes to science and medicine, and in America, music too.

In 1996, Sylvia and I were planning a trip to Italy. Three days before we were to leave, Sylvia remembered she needed to take her yearly mammogram. The next day, we got a call from the doctor. We had a meeting with her doctor and set up a biopsy, which confirmed that she had cancer in her left breast.

Two days later, she went to surgery at the Community Hospital of the Monterey Peninsula. I stayed at a hotel in Carmel. The operation went well. They removed all of her left breast and stripped the lymph nodes from her left arm. She spent three days in the hospital and was then sent home. She was weak and had to have a drainage tube in for the next two weeks. We returned to the hospital and had the tubes removed. In another week, she was back to work. She never worried about a reoccurrence.

I was the one who worried. But thank God the cancer never came back.

We flew into Milan in March of 1996. Milan is a very modern-looking city, with almost no historical buildings or monuments. It was bombed almost out of existence during WWII. Even the cathedral, originally built in 1365, was so destroyed that it was rebuilt after the war to look exactly like the original. Many visitors actually think this beautiful reproduction is the original.

VIEW FROM VENICE HOTEL

From Milan, we immediately went to Venice by train. We shared a compartment with a German couple and very much enjoyed talking to them. Arriving at the Venice train station, we gathered our luggage and walked out to the most amazing sight that we had ever seen: the Grand Canal in all its glory. Apart from the modern water taxis, what we saw was a canal

PIAZZA SAN MARCO, VENICE

that looked much the same as it had 800 years ago. It was so stunning that we just stood there for a few minutes taking in the view.

There were several ways to get to our hotel. We could take a gondola, or we could take a vaporetto (a water bus), or a water taxi. We hopped in the first water taxi that pulled alongside and the driver spoke very good English. "Where to?" he said.

"To the Londra Palace," Sylvia said.

That eight-minute ride to the hotel was without a doubt the most exciting sight that Sylvia and I had ever seen. All the wonderful cities we had seen over the years of travel to Europe dimmed in comparison. Venice is simply a work of art. It is in our opinion, then and now, the most incredible city on earth. We spent one week in a city where most folks will spend a few hours. Too bad, because they have missed a magical place that requires several days to absorb, and you still want more. It is not the largest, but the most impressive

Thaxton examines an unfinished work by Michelangelo.

church we have ever seen was the Basilica of San Marco in the square that bears its name.

After Venice, we traveled all over northern Italy. Our next stop was Florence, the birthplace of the Renaissance, the explosion of art and science after the Middle Ages. We spent five days in this incredible place. There is so much to see and appreciate in Florence. What impressed us most were the works of Michelangelo, especially *David*, and the Duomo, one of the largest churches in the world with its Baptistery that dates back to the fourth century. The only disappointment we could even mention was the amount of political graffiti on the buildings and walls of the city. In many of the older parts of major cities in Europe, there is graffiti on the historical structures. We attended mass at the SS Annunziata, a church dating back to 1481. Italy seems to be the only Western European country where people still attend church in numbers.

Sylvia in the Campo, Siena.

We visited Pisa, Siena, and Portofino, all wonderful places to spend time together. Then it was back to Milan for a few days before flying home.

Sylvia and a view of Tower Bridge, London.

Our visit to England and Scotland was memorable, too. We stayed at the Connaught, a beautiful but stuffy hotel. Frankly, it was hard for Sylvia or me to ask any staff member a question, as their attitude was so formal and reeked of superiority.

London is a beautiful city, with many wonderful historical places to see. The river Thames, around which the city developed over hundreds of years, is a good place to start. A boat trip down this river gives one a quick view of many of the historical sights, like the Tower Bridge, built in 1894, the Tower of London, and the like.

It is easy to walk around in London and a visit to Westminster Abbey is a must. But Sylvia and I truly enjoyed visiting Scotland more than England.

Our delight began with the train ride from London to Edinburgh. Most of the people in our car were from Scotland and were going home after a visit to London. About half the people would come up to us and ask what part of the States we were from. These folks were the friendliest we had met in any country we had visited in Western Europe. One young lady sitting across the aisle from us was with her sister and her baby of two or three months old. Sylvia struck up a conversation with this young woman. After a few minutes the woman excused herself to go to the restroom and she handed her baby to Sylvia to hold while she was away. I thought this was a very trusting thing to do.

We checked in at the Balmoral in Edinburgh, a huge, 200-year-old hotel. It was a far cry from the stuffiness of the London hotel. However, what awaited us was, with the exception of Venice, the most fascinating city we had yet visited.

AT THE GATEHOUSE, EDINBURGH CASTLE

Edinburgh Castle by itself was worth the trip. This castle has played an important role in Scottish history, both as a royal residence and as a military stronghold. It dates back to the 11th century. The Royal Mile was Sylvia's favorite. Located in the old town, the streets that make up the Royal Mile are Castlehill, Lawnmarket, High Street, Canongate, and Abbey Strand. There are shops for tourists, but the majority of the buildings date back centuries. It's like stepping back in time. Other attractions are the Scott Monument, Princes Street Gardens, the National Gallery, and the Royal Scottish Academy.

CHAPTER 13

Spain

Dr. Orestes del Castillo

When the Internet began to allow email, we stopped writing letters to Sylvia's cousins in Havana and started using email. Lina, her dear cousin, was married to Dr. Orestes del Castillo, who was an important person in the Castro government. He reported directly to Raul Castro himself. Because of his position, Dr. Orestes had his own Internet connection, including email. So for a good many years we had constant communication with Dr. Orestes and Lina. We never talked politics. There were so many other things to talk about. Sylvia had not seen her cousin Lina since they were teenagers in Havana, so they traded long emails and an occasional phone call about what was happening in their lives.

Dr. Orestes and I also had long discussions on what he was doing. His discipline was architecture and his assignment for Raul Castro was to restore Havana to its former glory—a daunting task, as Havana had deteriorated after the Revolution. It took him several years, but he managed to accomplish his goal of revitalizing the city. Dr. Orestes would send me photos of his progress.

SYLVIA AND HER COUSIN LINA.

Because of his position, he and Lina could travel without restrictions. In fact, all of their children had been educated abroad and were now living abroad. Orestes Jr. was an architect in Washington, D.C. Fexi and Javier were both contractors in Spain, and their daughter Mari Loli was a medical doctor in Spain.

Lina and Sylvia were talking on the phone and Sylvia suggested that she and Orestes meet us in Spain so that we could pay a visit to all the children (with the exception of Orestes Jr., who was in Washington). Orestes especially liked the idea, as he and I had grown to like and appreciate each other. So plans were made.

In August 2009, we arrived in Madrid. Sylvia and I spent one month in Spain. Madrid is a beautiful city. Without a doubt, it was the cleanest city we had seen in our many visits to Western Europe.

Sylvia and Natalia

On our first day, we met with Orestes and Lina, their children—Felix and his wife Olga and son Roco, Javier and his wife Natalia, and Mari Loli and her husband Adolfo and their six-year-old daughter, Claudia. We met in Javier and Natalia's apartment.

Sylvia had not seen her favorite cousin Lina in over fifty years. Sylvia and Lina were both overjoyed and in happy tears. Orestes and I had developed a respect for each other over the years and I found him a commanding presence. He had a good command of English, as did everyone there. We all drank wine and made toasts. For the next month, I was able to have nice visits with all. I was especially impressed with Lina and Orestes' daughter Mari Loli and her husband Adolfo. Both were medical doctors working for the Spanish government on various diseases such as diabetes. They both spoke English with little accent and were good-humored.

Sylvia was, rightly so, the center of attention. She spent hours bringing everyone up to date on her life after she'd left Cuba. While Sylvia and I spent much time with her relatives, we were still able to travel all over northern Spain, visiting walled cities.

We spent three days in San Sebastian, a city on the northern coast near France. Sylvia's grandparents had come from the Basque area of Spain and she especially wanted to go to San Sebastian, as it is located in the Basque Autonomous Community. It is also one of the most beautiful cities in Spain.

We visited Bilbao and the Guggenheim Museum, considered the most important structure of its time when it opened in 1997.

This was to be our last visit to Western Europe and in many respects, the best, thanks to Sylvia's wonderful family.

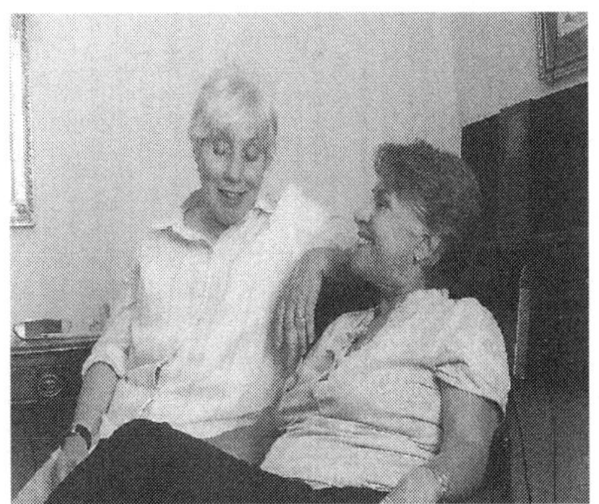

SYLVIA AND HER COUSIN LINA.

CHAPTER 14

Retirement

During the last ten years that Sylvia was working in Monterey County for the MCOE, I had been working as an oil painter, having retired from banking at the age of 58. I was reasonably successful selling my oils through the Marco Polo Galleria in Carmel. During that time, Sylvia was free each summer, as her contract allowed a summer vacation. We started visiting Europe every other year. First France, then Italy, then Austria—in fact, we visited almost every country in Western Europe.

By the time Sylvia was 65, we were still traveling to Europe and had made several trips to Venice, where I painted many oils of this incredible city. Now, however, she was at retirement age. She'd had a lifetime of helping people and children. As an excellent therapist and in my opinion, the best school psychologist in the county, she had nothing left to prove to herself or anyone. She had done God's work here on earth.

We were both getting older, and had a comfortable life with no real debt. Why not retire and enjoy life? We could continue to visit Europe; in fact, we still needed to visit the rest of England and Spain. At first, when I broached the subject, she rejected it, preferring to keep working. She had driven an average of 150 miles a day for 16 years without an accident. However, I was still worried every day, especially in the winter when it got dark at five o'clock. I also, selfishly, wanted to be with Sylvia all the time. We had both worked very hard and I really wanted to spend our senior years doing things together.

Then one night she almost had an accident. Only by quick thinking did she avoid a terrible crackup, which could have killed her. It was the final straw that changed her mind.

In fact, Sylvia was truly tired. She had done wonders with her life and now she also wanted to spend her senior years traveling with me. But her desire to serve her community didn't end at retirement.

Almost immediately, Sylvia wanted to join the Community Emergency Response Team (CERT). CERT teams are in almost every city in California. They are the people called on to help in any emergency such as large fires, earthquakes, search and rescue operations, terrorism, or any other kind of disaster. The program we participated in was extensive. We learned about disaster medical operations, how to establish treatment areas, and learned about conducting head-to-toe assessments of wounded victims, treating burns, fractures, and dislocation, splinting, nasal injuries, and hypothermia.

Our team would meet at the nearby fire station for classes, dry runs, and follow-up meetings. Each of us was given a backpack containing a green helmet with our name on it, goggles, a very bright yellow vest with orange stripes and the CERT emblem, a flashlight, duct tape, rubber gloves, work gloves, and a mask to help us breathe when the air is less than desirable, and last but not least, a whistle.

On dry runs, which were realistically staged, Sylvia was the calmest of us all. With her great memory, she never made a mistake. I had been a corpsman in the navy, and even with my knowledge, I would occasionally make a mistake and be corrected by the instructor. We were members of CERT for many years.

Sylvia amazed me every day I was with her. She had an upbeat spirit that would take on any challenge as long as she believed in it. She was also the nicest person to talk with. However, she could, on occasion, be assertive. I remember when I worked in banking and we were attending a bank function (a party). Sylvia was talking with an executive vice president. He had found out that she was from Cuba and thought it would be nice to say something good about Castro—a big mistake.

Sylvia listened for about two minutes and started in on this man. "You don't have a clue, do you? Castro killed thousands of Cubans, my best friend included. For God's sake, learn a little history."

The EVP turned pale. Sylvia stormed away from him and I thought my career was over. Later the man came up to Sylvia and me. To my surprise, he apologized to her. "I'm so sorry, my dear. I thought I was saying the right thing. You are right, he is a bad man and you had every right to bawl me out. I guess I've had too many drinks tonight. I'm truly sorry."

They hugged and I took a long breath of relief. I would keep my job. As it turned out, it was a feather in my cap. That same EVP came up to me later and praised Sylvia for her bravery in confronting him.

At another party, a lady was impressed by Sylvia and on being told of her being from Cuba, she said, "But you're so articulate. Were you a native princess?"

On one occasion, another woman asked Sylvia if she had come to the U.S. on a raft or small boat. Sylvia said, "No, I came on Pan Am."

These instances—and there were dozens—made me realize that many Americans don't know a thing about Cuba—or history, for that matter. But Sylvia never thought the same way I do; I never heard her complain about the ignorance of some folks. Unlike yours truly, who spent 35 years in banking and had sometimes had not the best view of my fellow man, and given the fact that she had been through hell and back as a teenager and young adult, she never showed any negative feeling toward people. I suspect that was the reason that she was so good at what she did. I also think that the great Creator gives some of us special talents that allow us to do His work on earth.

I know one thing for certain. With few exceptions, Sylvia played a necessary role in my successes as a banker and as a human being. She got the best out of me by setting an example to do the right thing every day of our marriage. I really had only one area where she couldn't help me. She could not paint my pictures for me. But I never painted anything that she didn't rave about.

Even though Sylvia was retired, she wanted to keep her licenses up to date. As a School Psychologist and Therapist, by regulation, she had to take nine college units each year. These subjects were meant to keep her up to date on the latest in testing and therapy. She could accomplish this by taking three all-day certified classes, which met these requirements.

One of the leading organizations that gives these day-long seminars is Family Services Agency of the Central Coast (FSACC), located in Santa Cruz. Sylvia took these seminars regularly, and got to know many of the instructors and managers. They offered her a part-time position as a therapist.

During her retirement, Sylvia worked two days a week for over six years as a therapist for families and individuals, many with problems related to drug or alcohol abuse. During those years, she saved many marriages and many individuals by putting them on the right track to a better, more productive and happy life.

CHAPTER 15

The Final Chapter

At the age of 72, Sylvia resigned from her final job. Her memory began to fail and she understood that there were difficulties coming.

For the next three years I was by her side. During the last year, we were confined to our home. For the last nine months I never left the house and was beside her every minute. Finally, she would not eat, and had to be taken to the hospital.

It was recommended by the hospital psychologist that Sylvia be placed in a facility that specialized in dealing with dementia, as I did not have the knowledge or the strength to care for her

24 hours a day, which is what she needed. I was down to 132 pounds and getting little sleep.

I was crushed with sorrow. I turned to my priest at our church, who relieved my guilt and helped me understand that this move was the right thing to do for both Sylvia and me. Sylvia needed round-the-clock knowledgeable care, which I was incapable of giving. I spoke with my closest friend, who agreed with my priest.

So the deed was done. I understand intellectually that I made the right decision. But emotionally, that's another story.

I close this book with these thoughts. I have had the most wonderful life I could ever imagine, thanks to Sylvia. She was and still is my hero—a human being who gave 100 percent to her husband, her work, and her life. If there has ever been a sinless human, it is she.

I have resigned myself to living with beautiful memories. I have wonderful friends who give me support, especially in our little community in the mountains. God bless my best friend and his wife. Those two wonderful people may never know just how much their efforts have sustained me through this ordeal.

God bless you, my darling and my love, my Sylvia.

THE END

About the Author

Nolan Thaxton Cordle was born in Atlanta, Georgia in 1937, and was what was described in those days as a "sickly kid." He spent most of his first seven years in the hospital, where he learned to draw.

After high school, he joined the Navy, where he became a medical illustrator, using watercolors to do large renderings of diseased organs and body parts for the interns' training sessions. After his hitch in the Navy, he settled in San Francisco, graduated from USF, and began a career in banking that lasted for more than 30 years. During that time, he met the love of his life, Sylvia, who became a school psychologist. They have been married for over 47 years and have lived in the Santa Cruz Mountains since 1978.

Visit his website to see the paintings he created on his voyages of discovery with Sylvia.

http://thaxtoncordle.wordpress.com

Made in the USA
Charleston, SC
19 February 2017